# *Surviving* POETRY

## Doors to Discovering Your Own Approach

Cynthia Parr

*University Partnership Centre,*
*Georgian College*

THOMSON
™
NELSON

Australia    Canada    Mexico    Singapore    Spain    United Kingdom    United States

**THOMSON**

**NELSON**

**Surviving Poetry: Doors to Discovering Your Own Approach**
Cynthia Parr

**Associate Vice President, Editorial Director:**
Evelyn Veitch

**Editor-in-Chief, Higher Education:**
Anne Williams

**Executive Editor:**
Laura MacLeod

**Marketing Manager:**
Shelly Collacutt Miller

**Developmental Editor:**
Theresa Fitzgerald

**Photo Researcher:**
Natalie Barrington

**Permissions Coordinator:**
Wendy Clark

**Production Manager:**
Cathy Deak

**Copy Editor:**
Tara Tovell

**Proofreader:**
Tara Tovell

**Production Coordinator:**
Ferial Suleman

**Design Director:**
Ken Phipps

**Interior Design:**
Katherine Strain

**Cover Design:**
Dianna Little

**Cover Image:**
C Squared Studios/Getty Images

**Compositor:**
Doris Chan

**Poem Design:**
Andrew Adams
William Bache
Eugene Lo
Peter Papayanakis
Peggy Rhodes
JJ Rivera
Katherine Strain
Glenn Toddun

**Printer:**
Thomson West

**Library and Archives Canada Cataloguing in Publication Data**

Parr, Cynthia

Surviving poetry : doors to discovering your own approach / Cynthia Parr.

ISBN 13: 978-0-17-610421-4
ISBN 10: 0-17-610421-6

1. Poetics—Textbooks.
2. Poetry—Explication—Textbooks.
I. Title.

PR502.P37 2007    808.1
C2007-900497-0

For Terry Whalen, who opened the doors for me.

# Contents

## DOOR #5 – TAKING IT WITH YOU: HOW DOES THIS POEM FIT INTO THE WORLD?

# Introduction

Poetry is a significant genre within the study of literature. Although it is a genre that can seem a bit intimidating, if we avoid or ignore poetry, we lose an enormous and fundamental part of the history, craftsmanship, and beauty of the recorded word available to us. This text introduces poetry by situating it in the context of your own experience. It presents short poems for you to work with and learn from before you move on to study other types of poetry, including the massive epics. The focus of the text is mainly on contemporary poetry, again just as a start that can help you to approach the more complex historic works at a later point in your studies. The text encourages you to find a "door" into poetry—a way to relate to this type of writing right now—and from there to continue on a path of vigorous study of the elements that make poetry so beautiful and different from other writing.

# Acknowledgments

Students, colleagues, friends, and relatives have contributed significantly to this project, and I consider them all invaluable co-authors. Thanks specifically to Laurentian at Georgian students in ENGL 1706 Fall 2004 and ENGL 1707 Winter 2006 for the inspiration; Blair Lesage for the photographs; Bruce Meyer for the advice; and Dave for his seemingly endless patience.

As well, many thanks to Anne Williams, Theresa Fitzgerald, Cathy Deak, Tara Tovell, and Angela Cluer and her design team, who have guided this text from concept to reality. The editors and the publisher would like to thank the following reviewers, who have provided much appreciated feedback: Neil Querengesser (Concordia University), Jonathon Penny (University of Lethbridge), and Lyn Bennet (Dalhousie University).

# DOOR #1
## ON THE DOORSTEP: WHY WRITE (OR READ) A POEM?

# The Poem as Photo

## YOUR PERCEPTION

You are sitting in a class or watching TV. Maybe you're talking with friends or family: Which topics always get your attention? Which issues do you feel strongly about? What really makes you angry? What always makes you laugh?

## THE CONCEPT

People write poetry because something in the world gets their attention. They see this object of their attention in a specific way and feel strongly enough to try to express their insight so that others will understand. Just as it can be interesting to hear others' ideas in conversation, it can be interesting to read others' ideas in poetry.

A poem is similar to a close-up photograph of life. It captures an observation of a moment or a detail, perceived through the writer's particular viewpoint or "lens." Whether we write it or read it, poetry can help us to sharpen our own perception of specific details. As the varied perspectives in the photos below indicate, the more closely we look at a moment in life—whether it is presented as a visual image or in words— the more we can learn about it.

Photos by: Blair Lesage

The first photo of The Great Wall of China gives us a sense of the environment surrounding the wall, but we can't see the wall well enough to understand what it really looks like. The second photo lets us see the wall itself, including stairs and a building, but it is still difficult to establish a personal connection with the wall because we are too far away from it. The third photo gives us a real sense of how it might feel to stand on the steps of the wall and walk into the structure at the top of it. In its intimate relationship with its subject matter, this photo resembles a poem: it invites us to connect with the details of a particular image that is important to the artist.

Because, like visual artists, writers of poetry look closely at life, poems are often compared to photographs, drawings, and paintings. The following two poem and photograph pairs provide examples of this similar perspective. These comparisons show that both photos and poetry can help us to notice and explore details we might otherwise overlook.

*My Son, My Executioner*

*My son, my executioner,*
*    I take you in my arms,*
*Quiet and small and just astir,*
*    And whom my body warms.*

5 *Sweet death, small son, our instrument*
*    Of immortality,*
*Your cries and hungers document*
*    Our bodily decay.*

*We twenty-five and twenty-two*
10 *    Who seemed to live forever,*
*Observe enduring life in you*
*    And start to die together.*

*by Donald Hall*

Photo by: Blair Lesage

In the poem, a young father speaks of one of the ways that his newborn son has affected his life. The father now perceives his own mortality because his son represents the generation that will outlive him and his wife. Realizing that his son is now the child and he himself is now the adult, the father is forced to look at his own life in the context of generational cycles.

In the photograph, the mother seems young herself, yet she carries the next generation in the form of the child attached to her back. Before the child was born, she may have moved more independently, but now the rest of her life will be affected by the presence of this child, and her perspective on the world will never be the same as it was before the child was born.

Both the poet and the photographer have captured a moment of the relationship between a parent and a child. Taking time to respond to or "read" both pieces carefully, we can appreciate the artists' detailed perspectives and make connections with and between their works.

Photo by: Blair Lesage

## We Wear the Mask

We wear the mask that grins and lies,

It hides our cheeks and shades our eyes –

This debt we pay to human guile;

With torn and bleeding hearts we smile,

And mouth with myriad subtleties.          5

Why should the world be over-wise,

In counting all our tears and sighs?

Nay, let them only see us, while

We wear the mask.

We smile, but O great Christ, our cries          10

To thee from tortured souls arise.

We sing, but oh the clay is vile

Beneath our feet, and long the mile;

But let the world dream otherwise,

We wear the mask!          15

*by Paul Laurence Dunbar*

Although the poem was written specifically about slavery, it also talks about the reality that may lie behind people's "public" faces—the way that some people conceal their true feelings by hiding behind a mask of artificial happiness. We may be able to think of someone we know who tries to appear happy, even when something is bothering him. We may not know what is behind his mask, or we may know him well enough to understand the reason he wears it. Connecting the poem to our own experience in this way helps us to gain a deeper understanding of its meaning.

In the photograph, we see a young girl staring straight at the camera. At first glance, she looks as if she may simply have been startled, but her eyes seem to speak of something deeper than her facial expression suggests. We can sense that she may have gone through experiences that have caused her to be afraid or unhappy.

Both the poet and the photographer have captured images of faces and have presented "close-ups" for us to consider. The outward expression of both faces gives us an initial impression, but the poet and photographer invite us to learn more about the human reality behind the surface of these faces.

As we practise identifying and giving meaning to specific details, we can open a door into understanding poetry.

## YOUR TURN

Find a photo that catches your attention and interest and write a response to it. Notice as many details as you can, and try to explain how the details influence your impressions.

# The Poem as Point of View

## YOUR PERCEPTION

How does your language change with what you are trying to say? When you're happy or really angry, how do you describe your feelings? How do you make it clear that you're joking, or that you're trying to express a serious idea?

## THE CONCEPT

Just as a photographer's perspective on the world is shaped by the particular lens and focus used, a poet's point of view can be expressed by using a speaker with a particular "voice." By taking on a persona, a poet can strengthen the ideas he or she is trying to express. For example, a male or female poet might speak as a father using harsh, clipped language to express bitterness about a war in which his child is involved. By taking on a different persona, however, that same poet could express a mother's patriotism and pride in her child's military service—a very different perspective on the subject of war.

Identifying the speaker in a poem can help you get closer to finding meaning within it, as this will help you to understand the perspective that the poet is adopting toward the poem's subject matter. In some cases, learning about poets' connections with their speakers can bring poetry to life: connecting writers' poetry to their own experiences and to their ideas can add a dimension of realism and help make their poetry more interesting.

In the following poem, Ted Hughes takes on the persona of a hawk in order to show us the way he sees this bird. The hawk is sure of its position in the hierarchy of nature, and Hughes makes this clear by letting the hawk speak for itself. If he had used another speaker to simply describe the hawk, we might not appreciate the bird's sense of absolute superiority.

# Hawk Roosting

I sit in the top of the wood, my eyes closed.
Inaction, no falsifying dream
Between my hooked head and hooked feet:
Or in sleep rehearse perfect kills and eat.

5  The convenience of the high trees!
The air's buoyancy and the sun's ray
Are of advantage to me;
And the earth's face upward for my inspection.

My feet are locked upon the rough bark.
10 It took the whole of Creation
To produce my foot, my each feather:
Now I hold Creation in my foot

Or fly up, and revolve it all slowly –
I kill where I please because it is all mine.
15 There is no sophistry in my body:
My manners are tearing off heads –

The allotment of death.
For the one path of my flight is direct
Through the bones of the living.
20 No arguments assert my right:

The sun is behind me.
Nothing has changed since I began.
My eye has permitted no change.
I am going to keep things like this.

BY TED HUGHES

# From
# Walking
# Both Sides of an
# Invisible
# Border

It is never easy
Walking with an invisible border
Separating my left and right foot

I feel like an illegitimate child
Forsaken by my parents        5
At least I can claim innocence
Since I did not ask to come
Into this world

Walking on both sides of this
Invisible border        10
Each and every day
And for the rest of my life
Is like having been
Sentenced to a torture chamber
Without having committed a crime        15

Understanding the history of humanity
I am not the least surprised
This is happening to me
A non-entity
During this population explosion        20
In a minuscule world

by Alootook Ipellie

In this excerpt, Alootook Ipellie speaks as someone who is placed between two worlds by his or her life situation and feels torn between them. If we know that, like the speaker, Ipellie is Inuit, and we learn something about the life of Inuit peoples, not only will we understand the poem better by connecting it to the poet's experiences, but we may also be able to identify with Ipellie's work more strongly, especially if we have shared similar experiences.

Each of us may recall and recount a moment in time differently: one person may find an incident exciting while another may find the same moment terrifying. Learning to see significant moments through eyes other than our own enriches and deepens our own perspective and makes us more interesting, as well as better-informed, human beings. We don't have to agree, or even to fully understand a perspective different from our own; just being willing to enter into and try to appreciate someone else's vision is an important step toward building bridges to other individuals and cultures. Poetry provides a multitude of visions with which we can experiment.

## YOUR TURN

Read two or more poems by the same author and identify the speaker in each. How is the difference between the poems emphasized by the choice of speaker? How would the meaning of the poems change if different speakers were used?

# The Poem as Song

## YOUR PERCEPTION

What is your favourite song? Why is it your favourite? If it has words, what is it about the lyrics that caught your attention the first time you heard it? If you didn't "get" the words the first time, why were you willing to play the song until the message was clear? Why do you like to listen to the song again and again?

## THE CONCEPT

Songs and poems have several things in common; often, in fact, songs are poems set to music. Both songs and poems capture a response to an event, an idea, a place, a person, or even a single word. They allow us to see something in detail and relate to it through the writer's eyes, and they both use sound, form, and rhythm as a framework for their ideas. The elements of songs and poems work together, sometimes seamlessly, as creative expressions that can make lasting impressions on those who hear or read them. Like a song, a poem can appeal to us on an intellectual or emotional level that we may not even be able to explain. Poems and songs are written from a very personal place, and they can be shared and enjoyed on that same personal level. If the writer's perception makes sense to us, the song or poem can become important to us: it can speak to us and even for us.

Even the songs we hear earliest in life have poetic elements: the rhythm, rhyme, and repetition of the following popular lullaby have made it a favourite with generations of families. We easily recognize the elements we respond to favourably in a song and enjoy hearing them again and again. Ironically, though, we sometimes respond less favourably to these same elements in poetry: finding doors to meaning in a poem can involve allowing ourselves to enjoy its musical elements.

# Hush, Little Baby

Hush, little baby, don't say a word.

Papa's gonna buy you a mockingbird

And if that mockingbird won't sing,

Papa's gonna buy you a diamond ring

5 And if that diamond ring turns brass,

Papa's gonna buy you a looking glass

And if that looking glass gets broke,

Papa's gonna buy you a billy goat

And if that billy goat won't pull,

10 Papa's gonna buy you a cart and bull

And if that cart and bull fall down,

You'll still be the sweetest little baby in town

# The Lonesome Death of Hattie Carroll

## by Bob Dylan

William Zanzinger killed poor Hattie Carroll
With a cane that he twirled around his diamond ring finger
At a Baltimore hotel society gath'rin'.
And the cops were called in and his weapon took from him
As they rode him in custody down to the station                    5
And booked William Zanzinger for first-degree murder.
But you who philosophize disgrace and criticize all fears,
Take the rag away from your face.
Now ain't the time for your tears.

William Zanzinger, who at twenty-four years                         10
Owns a tobacco farm of six hundred acres
With rich wealthy parents who provide and protect him
And high office relations in the politics of Maryland,
Reacted to his deed with a shrug of his shoulders
And swear words and sneering, and his tongue it was snarling.      15
In a matter of minutes on bail was out walking.
But you who philosophize disgrace and criticize all fears,
Take the rag away from your face.
Now ain't the time for your tears.

20    Hattie Carroll was a maid of the kitchen.
      She was fifty-one years old and gave birth to ten children
      Who carried the dishes and took out the garbage
      And never sat once at the head of the table
      And didn't even talk to the people at the table
25    Who just cleaned up all the food from the table
      And emptied the ashtrays on a whole other level,
      Got killed by a blow, lay slain by a cane
      That sailed through the air and came down through the room,
      Doomed and determined to destroy all the gentle.
30    And she never done nothing to William Zanzinger.
      But you who philosophize disgrace and criticize all fears,
      Take the rag away from your face.
      Now ain't the time for your tears.

      In the courtroom of honor, the judge pounded his gavel
35    To show that all's equal and that the courts are on the level
      And that the strings in the books ain't pulled and persuaded
      And that even the nobles get properly handled
      Once that the cops have chased after and caught 'em
      And that the ladder of law has no top and no bottom,
40    Stared at the person who killed for no reason
      Who just happened to be feelin' that way without warnin'.
      And he spoke through his cloak, most deep and distinguished,
      And handed out strongly, for penalty and repentance,
      William Zanzinger with a six-month sentence.
45    Oh, but you who philosophize disgrace and criticize all fears,
      Bury the rag deep in your face
      For now's the time for your tears.

These lines by Bob Dylan have been published as both a song and a poem. They tell a powerful story because of the way they are crafted: details are minimal but significant, and the repetition of the same lines at the end of each stanza provides a unifying idea. Looking carefully at the viewpoint expressed can help us to understand the very personal ideas behind the words; it can also help us to think about our own viewpoint and connect with the author's approach in a personal way.

## YOUR TURN

Choose lyrics from a favourite song. Discuss their meaning and specific ways that the writer expresses that meaning. How did you come to the impression you have of the song? Which of the lyrics are especially significant for you?

# Making Connections: Using Your Senses

## YOUR PERCEPTION

Have you ever tried to take in your surroundings using one sense at a time? This is an interesting exercise that can sharpen your ability to notice details. Try to notice all the sounds in a room, for example. There may be one that is dominant, but there are always others as well. Try to sort out those in the foreground from those in the background, and those that come and go from those that are persistent.

## THE CONCEPT

As we have seen so far, poetry invites us to look closely at details of the world, to understand diverse perspectives, and to appreciate passionate personal expression. Because it is a product of human creativity intended for human understanding, poetry uses language that relies heavily on the way that humans receive input from their environment—language rich with sensual impressions—so that, for example, we may "see" or—"smell" images presented in a poem. Becoming more keenly aware of our own senses can help us to identify and appreciate the sense-related details in poetry that are often so important to its meaning.

In the following poem, Hopkins expresses praise for variety—specifically for things with more than one colour. He asks us to picture several concrete items in nature (skies, trout, birds' wings), and then moves to broader, more abstract categories. Which things on earth are "counter," "original," "spare," and "strange"? We can participate in the poem by providing our own examples of beauty and diversity within these categories and the contrasts that follow them. Hopkins' appeal to our senses invites us to connect with his ideas as well as to explore our own.

Glory to be God for dappled things –
For skies of couple-colour as a brinded cow;
For rose-moles all in stipple upon trout that swim;
Fresh-firecoal chestnut-falls; finches' wings;
5  Landscape plotted and pieced – fold, fallow, and plough;
And áll trádes, their gear and tackle and trim.

All things counter, original, spare, strange;
Whatever is fickle, freckled (who knows how?)
With swift, slow; sweet, sour; adazzle, dim;
10  He fathers-forth whose beauty is past change:
Praise him.

All things counter, original, spare, strange;
Whatever is fickle, freckled (who knows how?)
With swift, slow; sweet, sour; adazzle, dim;
He fathers-forth whose beauty is past change:
Praise him.

# Bartok and the Geranium

by Dorothy Livesay

She lifts her green umbrellas
Towards the pane
Seeking her fill of sunlight
Or of rain;
Whatever falls                                                    5
She has no commentary
Accepts, extends,
Blows out her furbelows,
Her bustling boughs;

And all the while he whirls                                       10
Explodes in space,
Never content with this small room:
Not even can he be
Confined to sky
But must speed high and higher still                             15
From galaxy to galaxy,
Wrench from the stars their momentary notes
Steal music from the moon.

> She's daylight
> 20  He is dark
> She's heaven-held breath
> He storms and crackles
> Spits with hell's own spark.
>
> Yet in this room, this moment now
> 25  These together breathe and be:
> She, essence of serenity,
> He in a mad intensity
> Soars beyond sight
> Then hurls, lost Lucifer,
> 30  From heaven's height.
>
> And when he's done, he's out:
> She leans a lip against the glass
> And preens herself in light.

Dorothy Livesay uses a flower to represent a female in this poem, and the music of the composer Bartok to represent a male. She gives personalities to both the flower and the music, and asks us to imagine their different energies in the same room. Since we are given such a clear picture of the male and female, we may be able to think of people we know who are similar. Connecting with the male's whirling, exploding, speeding, and wrenching, and the female's lifting, seeking, accepting, and extending may help us to relate to the poem as we explore its meaning.

## YOUR TURN

Describe one of your favourite places in terms of your senses. Try to express how you respond to the place by describing detailed sensual impressions that others will be able to appreciate.

# DOOR #2
## WHAT IS THIS POEM ABOUT?

# Words That Stand Out

## YOUR PERCEPTION

When you think of excitement, which words come to mind? Which words would you use to describe contentment? What does the word "rumble" make you think about? How about the word "ticking"? Do certain words trigger particular responses in you?

## THE CONCEPT

Understanding a poem does not have to begin with a deep analysis of its rhyme or rhythm. Nor does unlocking the meaning of a poem have to involve comparing it with other, similar poems. Although these approaches may help an experienced reader to find meaning, there are other ways of beginning to respond to a poem that work just as well. Use a method you are comfortable with to get started with a poem. Asking even the most basic questions is fine—you can move from there to a more detailed consideration as you gain an understanding of some of the ways that poems work.

You might start by asking questions such as, "What is the poem talking about? Who or what is mentioned in the poem? What happens to that person or thing?" Once you have answered these basic questions about the poem's content, you can start to look at individual words and phrases. Sometimes a poet will use several words that can be connected to one another in some way (for example, through the various ways they describe one thing). Grouping these words can help to uncover focal points that the poet has created in a poem. At other times, a poet will use exact repetitions of words or phrases to create an emphasis that may provide a specific key to the poem's meaning.

# THE SHARK

He seemed to know the harbour,
So leisurely he swam;
His fin,
Like a piece of sheet-iron,
5    Three-cornered,
And with knife-edge,
Stirred not a bubble
As it moved
With is base-line on the water.

10  His body was tubular
And tapered
And smoke-blue,
And as he passed the wharf
He turned,
15  And snapped at a flat-fish
That was dead and floating.
And I saw the flash of a white throat,
And a double row of white teeth,
And eyes of metallic grey,
20  Hard and narrow and slit.

Then out of the harbour,
With that three-cornered fin
Shearing without a bubble the water
Lithely,
25  Leisurely,
He swam—
That strange fish,
Tubular, tapered, smoke-blue,
Part vulture, part wolf,
30  Part neither—for his blood was cold.

by E. J. Pratt

In this poem, a shark swims through a harbour. We sense that the shark is dangerous, with its "double row of white teeth,/ And eyes of metallic grey,/ Hard and narrow and slit." But Pratt does even more with his choice of words: "sheet-iron," "knife-edge," "base-line," "tubular," "tapered," "smoke-blue," and "shearing" all seem to describe something metallic and cold. Perhaps Pratt is comparing the shark to a submarine or a torpedo and thus emphasizing the danger the shark embodies. Identifying and grouping similar words in this way can help us to understand the imagery used to show the threat the shark poses.

# Do Not Go Gentle into That Good Night

Do not go gentle into that good night,
Old age should burn and rave at close of day;
Rage, rage against the dying of the light.

Though wise men at their end know dark is right,
Because their words had forked no lightning they   5
Do not go gentle into that good night.

Good men, the last wave by, crying how bright
Their frail deeds might have danced in a green bay,
Rage, rage against the dying of the light.

Wild men who caught and sang the sun in flight,   10
And learn, too late, they grieved it on its way,
Do not go gentle into that good night.

Grave men, near death, who see with blinding sight
Blind eyes could blaze like meteors and be gay,
Rage, rage against the dying of the light.   15

And you, my father, there on the sad height,
Curse, bless, me now with your fierce tears, I pray.
Do not go gentle into that good night.
Rage, rage against the dying of the light.

*by Dylan Thomas*

Dylan Thomas wrote this poem when his father was dying. Several types of men are mentioned—"wise," "good," "wild," and "grave"—and the poem contains some repetition of the words "night" and "light." Two lines are repeated throughout: "Do not go gentle into that good night" and "Rage, rage against the dying of the light" each appear four times in only eighteen lines. This repetition alone indicates that these lines contain important ideas, and by focusing on them, we can start to unlock the meaning of the poem. Images of darkness, such as night, are often related to death, and images of light are often related to life. Thus, by pleading with his father not to go willingly into the darkness of night, Thomas asks his father to object to death—not simply to give in, but rather to react against and resist the idea of leaving the light of the earthly world. If we understand this to be a key idea in the poem, we can make sense of the rest of the poem by relating the wise, good, wild, and grave men to this resistance.

## YOUR TURN

Choose a poem to study. Begin by asking, "What is this poem about?" List or underline the things, people, or places mentioned and what they do in the poem. Then look for groups of similar words and for repetition. Can you determine the focus of the poem?

# Words We Think We Know, but May Not

## YOUR PERCEPTION

Snow, slush, ice, freezing rain, ice pellets, hail, flurries, and snow squalls are all words used to describe elements of winter weather. What is the difference among these words? What exact conditions does each word describe?

## THE CONCEPT

If you have ever used a thesaurus, you know that in English there are often several words that can have approximately, but not exactly, the same meaning. You may have received comments on some of your writing about your word usage, indicating that one word you have chosen does not work quite as well as another, similar word would. Choosing words to say exactly what we mean is part of clear communication, in academic or any other type of writing.

Poets must choose their words with exactitude as well. "Close enough" won't do for a poet—she has to know what she is trying to say and choose the most effective and exact words to convey each thought. When we read poetry, we can assume that each word is used for a specific reason: there are no fillers or accidental words.

If we are going to unlock the meaning of a poem, we need to understand each word in it. This process includes realizing that words can be used in more than one way, and being willing to use a dictionary to look up the possible meanings of words we are not sure of. Sometimes a poet will use a familiar word in an unfamiliar way, so it is worth checking for alternate meanings even of the words we think we know.

# A Noiseless Patient Spider

A noiseless patient spider,
I mark'd where on a little promontory it stood isolated,
Mark'd how to explore the vacant vast surrounding,
It launch'd forth filament, filament, filament, out of itself,
5   Ever unreeling them–ever tirelessly speeding them.

And you O my Soul where you stand,
Surrounded, detached, in measureless oceans of space,
Ceaselessly musing, venturing, throwing, seeking the spheres to connect them,
Till the bridge you will need be form'd, till the ductile anchor hold,
10   Till the gossamer thread you fling catch somewhere, O my Soul.

by Walt Whitman

Unfamiliar words in this poem may include "mark'd," "promontory," "filament," "musing," "ductile," and "gossamer." If we look up the word "mark'd" in a dictionary, we won't find it in that exact form. The root or core word in "mark'd" is "mark." According to the *ITP Nelson Canadian Dictionary of the English Language*, there are eighteen different ways that "mark" can be used as a noun (i.e., a person, place, or thing). In this poem however, the speaker says, "I mark'd where, ..." so we know that "mark" is used as a verb (i.e., an action), and fortunately for us, the dictionary provides only six definitions for this word as a verb:

> —*v.* **marked, marking, marks.** —*tr.* **1.** To make a visible trace or impression on, as with a spot, line, or dent. **2.** To single out or indicate by or as if by a mark. **3.** To set off or separate by or as if by a line or boundary: *marked off our property.* **4.** To attach or affix identification, such as a price tag, to. **5.** To evaluate (academic work) according to a scale of letters and numbers. **6.** To give attention to; notice.

Of the definitions of "mark" listed here, the one that fits best with the way the word is used in the poem is 6.: "to give attention to; notice." The poem could read, "I noticed where, on a little ..." and it would make sense.

To find an appropriate meaning, then, for an unfamiliar word, try these steps:

1. Find the root of the word and look that up (other forms of the word will be listed in the definition).
2. Identify the way that the word is used in the poem (as a noun or verb, etc.).
3. Find a use of the word that can be substituted in the poem to make sense.

At this point, you may be wondering why a poet would use a word as unusual as "mark'd" when he could have just said "noticed"! Poets use the language of their times, the language of particular types of poetry, and sometimes language that is intended to stand out and catch the reader's attention. Part of unlocking the meaning of a poem is taking the time to appreciate the word choices the poet makes. Once we learn the meanings of the unfamiliar words, we can start to make connections among them and to make sense of the poem.

If we looked up the other possibly unfamiliar words Whitman has chosen, we would find that the following definitions fit well with the way the words are used in the poem:

promontory: "a high ridge of land or rock jutting out into a body of water; a headland"

filament: "a fine or thinly spun thread, fibre, or wire"

muse (root of musing): "to be absorbed in one's thoughts, engage in meditation"

ductile: "easily moulded or shaped" or "capable of being readily persuaded or influenced"

gossamer: "sheer, light, delicate, or tenuous"

Just by inserting these senses of the words into the poem, we can start to build a better understanding of what it is about.

The other types of words we should look up in the dictionary are those that seem familiar but that may have more than one meaning. If a familiar word does not seem to make sense in a poem, consider looking it up to find other possible meanings. For example, the word "speeding" in this poem does not make sense if it means "rushing" or "exceeding the speed limit." In the poem, the spider is unreeling filaments from itself, "ever tirelessly speeding them." The definitions of "speed" as a verb include "to further, promote, or expedite"—in other words, to get something done. This definition makes sense in the context of the poem, and we can thus understand that the spider is producing the filaments willingly and tirelessly.

## YOUR TURN

Determine the exact meaning of the unfamiliar words in a poem by exploring their definitions in a dictionary. Let the various senses of key words influence your ideas about the meaning of the poem: could these words suggest more than one interpretation?

# Working with Imagery

## YOUR PERCEPTION

Look around you and choose five words that best describe your surroundings right now. Assume that you have to describe your environment in exact terms to someone who isn't with you. How specific can you make each word?

## THE CONCEPT

Because poets want to help us understand their ideas, they choose their words and craft their lines in specific ways to help us appreciate what they have seen or thought. As we have seen, the words they select often relate to our senses. When we can pick out specific words and phrases that create sensual impressions in a poem—in other words, the poem's imagery—we can begin to understand some of the choices the poet made in order to communicate her ideas. If we can understand some of those choices, we can begin to make sense of the poem's meaning.

## you fit into me
### by Margaret Atwood

you fit into me
like a hook into an eye

a fish hook
an open eye

This poem has only sixteen words, so we might be surprised by the power of its imagery. The first two lines present an image of two people ("you" and "me") fitting together like a fastener with two parts (a hook and an eye). Hooks and eyes complement each other and work to hold something together. The words used in the first two lines thus imply a positive relationship between the two people, but the tone of the poem changes entirely when the words "fish" and "open" are added in the next two lines. The image of the fish hook suggests something barbed and dangerous, while the open eye evokes something vulnerable. With this brief, two-word clarification, the relationship between "you" and "me" takes on a completely different, much more negative quality. Thus, despite its brief length, this poem makes a strong statement through its effective imagery.

by e. e. cummings

in Just-
spring          when the world is mudluscious the little
lame balloonman

whistles      far     and wee                                    5

and eddieandbill come
running from marbles and
piracies and it's
spring

when the world is puddle-wonderful                               10

the queer
old balloonman whistles
far        and        wee
and bettyandisbel come dancing
from hop-scotch and jump-rope and                                15

it's
spring
and
    the
        goat-footed                                              20

balloonMan          whistles
far
and
wee

This poem paints a picture of children playing outside on a spring day. Some of the words that contribute to that picture include "balloonman," "marbles," "piracies," "hopscotch," and "jump-rope," words associated with games that children play outdoors. Cummings also combines words to create new ones such as "mudluscious" and "puddlewonderful," both of which give us a sense of the pleasure children feel when they are finally able to play outside unfettered after a long, cold winter. The pairs of names ("eddieandbill" and "bettyandisbel") suggest friendships between children who are inseparable. By using all of this imagery, e. e. cummings creates a picture not just of any spring day, but of all the joy and freedom children can experience in the spring.

Although individual readers may attach slightly different associations to particular words in a poem, the most common or shared interpretations of a poem tend to be formed by focusing on its imagery. Students just beginning to read poetry are often concerned about forming the "right" interpretation or, on the other hand, about having their own interpretations challenged. While it is difficult to define what makes an interpretation "wrong," a reader can get off track by not paying close enough attention to the way in which images are presented in a poem. For example, if you thought that in cummings' poem pirates were invading a park and chasing a heavy-set old man, this interpretation wouldn't make sense in the context of the actual words used in the poem. The word used is "piracies," (having nothing to do here with actual pirates), a "balloonman" sells balloons (rather than looking like a balloon), and he whistles because it's spring (not because he is out of breath from being chased). Skilled poetic interpretation grows from experience with the limitations as well as the possibilities of meaning suggested in a poem's lines.

## YOUR TURN

Choose an event or an object. Describe it by providing several images that create a specific impression of it. Then choose a different group of words to create an entirely different impression of the same event or object. Test your imagery by asking someone else to tell you what she pictures when she reads both sets of words.

# Making Connections: Your Reading Process

## YOUR PERCEPTION

How long does it take someone to get to know you? Is one conversation in class, for example, enough for a person to get a full, fair impression of your personality? In how many situations should the person see you before he really knows who you are?

## THE CONCEPT

Just as it takes a while to get to know another person well, it may also take a while to get to know a poem well. Although there are many ways to do this, reading with a specific purpose in mind each time we go through a poem usually works well. For example, the first time we read a poem, we might just enjoy its sounds. The next time, we might notice details that stand out and catch our attention. Then, we might be ready to look for other specific elements in the poem that we know will help us to unlock its meaning.

As you read the following poems, try to be aware of the process you go through to understand what they mean. Notice what you do each time you read the first poem and then adjust it slightly for the second poem: does the sequence work better one way rather than the other? Which tools are you developing already that give you some confidence with a new poem?

Often, moving from a broad, general reading to a more specific analysis works well. When you are ready to attend to the details in the following poems, be sure to consider the word choice, the unfamiliar vocabulary, and the imagery used in both. The questions following the poems may help you to focus on the process you use to unlock their meanings.

# Dark Pines under Water

*by Gwendolyn MacEwan*

The land like a mirror turns you inward
And you become a forest in a furtive lake;
The dark pines of your mind reach downward,
You dream in the green of your time,
5  Your memory is a row of sinking pines.

Explorer, you tell yourself this is not what you came for
Although it is good here, and green;
You had meant to move with a kind of largeness,
You had planned a heavy grace, an anguished dream.

10  But the dark pines of your mind dip deeper
And you are sinking, sinking, sleeper
In an elementary world;
There is something down there and you want it told.

1. What is this poem about? Who is doing or saying what?
2. Who is the speaker in the poem? What is his or her point of view?
3. Which words in this poem stand out for you?
4. Can you identify groupings or repetitions of words?
5. Which words do you need to look up?
6. What imagery is used? What impressions does this imagery create?
7. How can someone "become a forest in a furtive lake"?
8. What is "the green of your time"? What ideas or meanings can you connect with the word "green"?
9. How can someone "move … with largeness"?
10. Why would someone plan to have a "heavy grace, an anguished dream"?
11. What is an "elementary world"?
12. Why might someone want something from deep inside him- or herself to be told?

# Winter Song

by Elizabeth Tollet

Ask me no more, my truth to prove,
What I would suffer for my love.
With thee I would in exile go
To regions of eternal snow,
O'er floods by solid ice confined,                    5
Through forest bare with northern wind:
While all around my eyes I cast,
Where all is wild and all is waste.
If there the tim'rous stag you chase,
Or rouse to fight a fiercer race,                     10
Undaunted I thy arms would bear,
And give thy hand the hunter's spear.
When the low sun withdraws his light,
And menaces an half-year's night,
The conscious moon and stars above                    15
Shall guide me with my wand'ring love.
Beneath the mountain's hollow brow,
Or in its rocky cells below,
Thy rural feast I would provide,
Nor envy palaces their pride.                         20
The softest moss should dress thy bed,
With savage spoils about thee spread:
While faithful love the watch should keep,
To banish danger from thy sleep.

1. What is this poem about? Who is doing or saying what?
2. Who is the speaker in the poem? What is his or her point of view?
3. Which words in this poem stand out for you?
4. Can you identify groupings or repetitions of words?
5. Which words do you need to look up in the dictionary?
6. What imagery is used? What impressions does this imagery create?
7. Can you see a purpose for the first two lines of the poem?
8. What would the speaker do to prove his or her love to the hunter?
9. What does it mean to "keep watch"?
10. Which qualities does the poet associate with hunting and hunters?
11. Which qualities does the poet associate with the speaker?
12. Why is this poem entitled "Winter Song"?

## YOUR TURN

Choose a poem you haven't read before. Record the process you follow to unlock the door to its meaning and identify those steps that are most useful in this process. Detail how far you get with your unlocking process: are you satisfied, or do you need more keys?

# DOOR #3
## WHAT IS THIS POEM SAYING?

# Punctuation and Layout

## YOUR PERCEPTION

When you listen to a professor in class who speaks more slowly than you do, how do you react? Does his pacing help you to relax and think more carefully, or do you find yourself waiting impatiently for the next word to complete his thoughts? How do we know when a speaker has finished one idea and is ready to move on to the next? What signals does a speaker give when she is going to move quickly or take a while to make a point?

## THE CONCEPT

Like speakers, poets can use signals to organize ideas and influence their pacing. Punctuation marks (the "street signs" of literature) can help us to navigate through the lines of a poem, telling us where ideas begin and end, and how quickly to read them. Poets use commas, periods, colons, dashes, and all the other punctuation marks for very specific reasons, and when we learn to read them, as well as the words in a poem, we can discover more clues to meaning. In addition to using punctuation marks as signals, poets can also use the layout of a poem to indicate its ideas and pacing. Breaking up one idea into several lines, for example, can call attention to particular groupings of words and force us to read through them slowly.

# The Wheel

## by Wendell Berry

At the first strokes of the fiddle bow
the dancers rise from their seats.
The dance begins to shape itself
in the crowd, as couples join,

5    and couples join couples, their movement
together lightening their feet.
They move in the ancient circle
of the dance. The dance and the song
call each other into being. Soon

10   they are one – rapt in a single
rapture, so that even the night
has its clarity, and time
is the wheel that brings it round.
In this rapture the dead return.

15   Sorrow is gone from them.
They are light. They step
into the steps of the living
and turn with them in the dance
in the sweet enclosure

20   of the song, and timeless
is the wheel that brings it round.

Sometimes when we read a poem aloud, we tend to stop at the end of each line, as if the end of a line indicates the end of an idea. But because each line in a poem is not necessarily a sentence, we often need to continue reading through the line breaks (the ends of the lines) until the poet shows us, with punctuation, that an idea has ended. In Wendell Berry's poem, for example, the first idea is two lines long. The first word begins with a capital letter, and then there is no punctuation until the period after the word "seats." The second idea in the poem is even longer, beginning with the word "The" and ending with the word "feet." The commas in the middle of this idea, as well as the line breaks, organize the movement of the couples joining the dance, but the complete idea doesn't end (with a period) until its fourth line. Two individual lines in this poem are complete sentences: "In this rapture the dead return." and "Sorrow is gone from them." Because ideas are often not completed in single lines of poetry, we can assume that by phrasing these ideas this way, Berry wants to call our attention to them. If we understand this signal, we can gather that the return of the dead to dance with the living is significant to the meaning of the poem.

# The White Lilies
## by Louise Gluck

As a man and woman make
a garden between them like
a bed of stars, here
they linger in the summer evening
and the evening turns                                     5
cold with their terror: it
could all end, it is capable
of devastation. All, all
can be lost, through scented air
the narrow columns                                      10
uselessly rising, and beyond,
a churning sea of poppies—

Hush, beloved. It doesn't matter to me
how many summers I live to return:
this one summer we have entered eternity.              15
I felt your two hands
bury me to release its splendor.

The first idea in this poem is seven-and-a-half lines long! It begins with the image of love as a garden and ends with an image of potential devastation. The idea that the love shared by the poem's man and woman could end is presented slowly, with minimal punctuation and frequent line breaks, as if it evolves. Thus, we are given time to see the progression from the couple's appreciation of each other and a star-lit summer evening to their experience of cold terror at the possibility of their love's future destruction. If Louise Gluck had simply expressed the man and woman's fear in the first line, we would have missed learning about the context and the significance of their fear. By using line breaks to spread the idea over several lines, however, Gluck allows us to slow down and participate in the feelings of the couple. In contrast, later in the poem, the phrase, "Hush, beloved," is short, quick, and direct, with only two words included before the final period. This gives us a sense of action and intent—that one of the members of the couple wants the fear to end and is going to present another idea that will put the fear into perspective. Learning to notice and interpret Gluck's use of punctuation and line breaks in this poem thus helps us to find subtle indications of its meaning.

## YOUR RESPONSE

Choose a poem that uses punctuation and rewrite its ideas in complete sentences. Note where all the punctuation is used, and think about why the poet's words may be organized in this particular way. When you reread the poem in its original layout, can you now see how the punctuation and the structure of the lines give clues to the poem's meaning?

# Theme

## YOUR PERCEPTION

What do you and your friends or family talk about? Are the topics seasonal, such as who will win a sports trophy? Are the topics personal, such as the ways that you interact with one another? Do you talk about current events, distant history, or dreams?

## THE CONCEPT

Like conversations among those who share an understanding, poetry often focuses on topics that are common in human experience. These include an appreciation of nature, our perceptions of ourselves and one another, relationships, death, etc. A poet's particular perspective on a poem's topic indicates the theme of the poem, and identifying this theme can help us to see an issue in our own life and world in a new way. If we have strong feelings for someone, for example, a poet may provide a specific description of the joy or pain of love that clarifies our feelings exactly. Comparing different poets' perspectives on the same topic by identifying the themes within their poems may broaden and help to clarify our own perspective even more. Developing the ability to identify a theme in a poem is another key to unlocking its meaning.

One of the topics mentioned in Door #1 is war. Because war is a subject that affects so many people in so many countries, it inspires frequent responses from poets, such as the following two poems.

# War Movie in Reverse

by Mark Johnston

Holes close to smooth skin
when the shrapnel flashes out.
The shores of burns recede,
and flames leap with their hot metal
5    back into the bomb that rises,
whole and air-borne again,
with its gathered blast.
Leading the plane perfectly,
the bomb arcs back slowly
10   through the open gates
and disappears into the waiting belly.
The bombardier lifts
his peering eye from the sight.
Swallowing its wake,
15   the plane returns to base
with its countermanded mission.
The pilot, irresolute now, faces
his commandant, who marches,
brisk and backward
20   to the general's lair.
The general takes back the orders.
But into what deep and good and hidden
recess of the will
go his thoughts of not bombing?

 

One of the challenges of reading poetry can be to put aside our emotional response to a topic and to focus on a poem's message—or theme—instead. Refusing to read a poem simply because it is about war, for example, without learning what the poet is going to *say* about war, can limit an opportunity to broaden our perspective on this subject. Discovering a poet's perspective, however, is not always easy: sometimes we have to make connections among the details provided by the poet in order to piece together its theme. In the above poem, for example, Mark

Johnston describes a bombing backwards: this allows us to focus on the progression of images and events and to think about the causes of each one. When we finally get back to the general who gave the order for the bombing, Johnston ends the poem with a question that he seems unable or unwilling to answer. Is he saying that the general has no will to abstain from bombing? If so, he may be making a statement about the reoccurrence of war, and the poem's theme may be war's inevitability when power is in the wrong hands.

# Mr. Polk Was Afraid of the Rain

*by Adam Sol*

No damage we did to his garden would bring him out of doors
if the slightest drizzle leaked off his rusty roof. After a while,
beheading his tulips got boring so we'd fetch his paper for a
        penny.
He didn't mind us dripping on the carpet.                                    5

> *I have been to the meadow,*
> *I have been to the shore,*
> *I have been to the ghetto,*
> *I have been to the war.*

One stormy November weekend my mother tsked                                  10
and brought him bread and eggs. He repaid us
with shortbread so buttery it slipped through our fingers.

> *I have seen the boys bite,*
> *I have seen the boys lie,*
> *I have seen the boys fight,*                                               15
> *I have seen the boys die.*

Once when I came home whistling
a glory hymn we sang in school, Mr. Polk
beaned me with a half-eaten apple. From twenty yards.

> *I once knew a Thomas,*                                                     20
> *I once knew two Jacks,*
> *They went out in August,*
> *They came home in sacks.*

When I was old enough to join, I knocked on his door
to show him the uniform. He brought me inside                                25
holding my elbow like he was helping an old
woman cross the street. Showed me
his medals and trophies: two stars, a fistful of ribbons,
and a tooth inside a velvet ringbox.

> *Thomas was hit in the heart,*                                             30
> *Jack was hit in the brain,*
> *The other Jack was blown apart,*
> *They all were hit in the rain.*

In this poem, a young boy's thoughts alternate with those of Mr. Polk, a veteran of a war. We are able to piece together Mr. Polk's feelings about the war he participated in through his memories expressed in every other stanza, spoken in rhyme. When, by the end of the poem, we learn the circumstances in which all of Mr. Polk's comrades-in-arms were killed, we understand why, as indicated at the beginning, he won't go outdoors in the rain. Thus, a strongly expressed theme of Adam Sol's poem is the lasting pain that involvement in a war can cause. What other themes does his poem suggest?

## YOUR TURN

Choose a poem that approaches a topic common to human experience. Use all the keys you have gained so far to unlock the meaning or theme(s) of the poem and draw some conclusions about the poet's approach to the topic.

# Tone

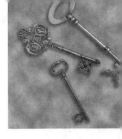

## YOUR PERCEPTION

Have you ever heard the saying, "It's not what you say as much as how you say it that counts"? Has anyone ever criticized your tone of voice? Do you know someone who whines? Have you ever heard someone who can make the words "Good morning" sound scary?

## THE CONCEPT

Just as we hear more than only the words when someone speaks, we can read more than just the words when a poet writes. We have seen that a poet can make a statement about a topic by expressing a particular perspective, thus conveying the poem's theme. We have also seen, in Door #1, that a poet can use a speaker (or persona) to make this theme more personal. The speaker's attitude or tone of voice, generated by the poet's choice of words, can provide important clues to the meaning or theme(s) in a poem.

In the following poem, Rena Williams takes on the persona of a man or woman who sees his or her brother for the first time in fifteen years. The speaker alternates between using "you" and "he" to describe the brother, as if to emphasize the distance between the two siblings. The speaker adopts a negative tone when describing the brother by using words ("ugly," "drunkard," "plodded," "drifts," and "mister") that suggest a harsh appraisal and perhaps some resentment. Yet, the words connecting the siblings to their grandmother ("skated," "dodging," "enough for everyone," "shouted that space to life," and "missing") set a more positive tone. And in the last stanza, we can see that the speaker retains some affection for the brother and is the only person who can see through his ugliness to appreciate his true personality. Through the words of her speaker, Williams thus establishes a tone that suggests the complex relationships siblings can sometimes share.

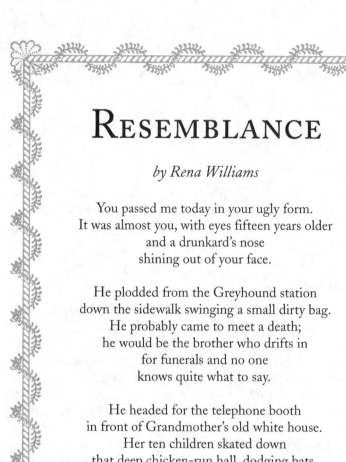

# RESEMBLANCE

*by Rena Williams*

You passed me today in your ugly form.
It was almost you, with eyes fifteen years older
and a drunkard's nose
shining out of your face.

5     He plodded from the Greyhound station
down the sidewalk swinging a small dirty bag.
He probably came to meet a death;
he would be the brother who drifts in
for funerals and no one
10     knows quite what to say.

He headed for the telephone booth
in front of Grandmother's old white house.
Her ten children skated down
that deep chicken-run hall, dodging bats.
15     Four interchangeable cubicles, enough for everyone,
opened into that hall which bristled,
bled with our scabby knees. We shouted
that space to life.

So you walk by in your ugly form
20     and I end missing my grandmother and the bats.
Students live there now, they've painted
LOVE on every sagging window, LOVE
in every purple shade and shape, and they
will not repeal a contrast so complete.

25     I watched you, mister, I know you well
and I'm the only person in this town
glad to see you.

# The Exchange

by Alicia Ostriker

I am watching a woman swim below the surface
Of the canal, her powerful body shimmering,
Opalescent, her black hair wavering
Like weeds. She does not need to breathe. She faces

Upward, keeping abreast of our rented canoe.
Sweet, thick, white, the blossoms of the locust trees          5
Cast their fragrance. A redwing blackbird flies
Across the sluggish water. My children paddle.

If I dive down, if she climbs into the boat,
Wet, wordless, she will strangle my children
And throw their limp bodies into the stream.          10
Skin dripping, she will take my car, drive home.

When my husband answers the doorbell and sees
This magnificent naked woman, bits of sunlight
Glittering on her pubic fur, her muscular
Arm will surround his neck, once for each insult          15

Endured. He will see the blackbird in her eye,
Her drying mouth incapable of speech,
And I, having exchanged with her, will swim
Away, in the cool water, out of reach.

20

In this poem, Alicia Ostriker uses a tone that has multiple shades: the calm opening, followed by the angry fantasy of action, ending with the achievement of untroubled separation. We can gather from this poem that the speaker is having some trouble with her family. She fantasizes about switching places with an imaginary woman who she sees swimming in the water beside her canoe. The language related to the water woman before the switch—when she is distant, below the water's surface, where the speaker longs to be—includes words such as "shimmering," "opalescent," "wavering," "sweet," and "fragrance," all of which create a sense of beauty and a calm tone. In contrast, the language related to the water woman after the speaker's fantasized switch has taken place includes words such as "strangle," "throw," "muscular," "surround," and "drying mouth," which suggest her silent power that is expressed through action rather than empty speech. These words thus inject an angry tone into the central portion of the poem. And although we may not be sure exactly what the speaker would like to have happen (for she says "If" she dives down), her tone at the end of the poem is clear. The last line conveys a sense of calm, detached relief, when the speaker has removed herself from her family and can remain "in the cool water, out of reach."

## YOUR TURN

Choose a poem that has an obvious topic and speaker. Identify the poem's theme and consider the specific details of the poem that suggest and support this theme. In particular, note how the speaker's tone is established through the poet's choice of words.

# Making Connections: In Your Own Words

## YOUR PERCEPTION

Do you ever paraphrase someone's words or ask questions in order to understand someone better? When you're studying for a test or exam, do you rewrite your notes from class in your own words so that they're easier to work with? If a professor makes a point that you're not quite sure about, do you ask for clarification?

## THE CONCEPT

Just as we can communicate with another person in order to understand his or her ideas, we can communicate with a poem to discover its meaning. A great way to find meaning in a poem is to put it into your own words and "talk" to it. This may sound strange since so much emphasis is generally placed on a poem's specific words, phrases, and layout, but sometimes it is difficult to appreciate all of those details until we can identify with a poem personally. Just by reorganizing a poem temporarily, we can see its ideas more clearly and start to appreciate some of the choices made by the poet in expressing those ideas. Once we have used reorganization and paraphrasing to form an understanding of what a poem is saying on a basic level, then we can put the poem back together in its original form and appreciate its unique language and detail more fully.

# The Anniversary

by Ai

You raise the ax,
the block of wood screams in half,
while I lift the sack of flour
and carry it into the house.

5   I'm not afraid of the blade
you've just pointed at my head.
If I were dead, you could take the boy,
hunt, kiss gnats, instead of my moist lips.
Take it easy, squabs are roasting,

10   corn, still in husks, crackles,
as the boy dances around the table:
old guest at a wedding party for two sad-faced clowns,
who together, never won a round of anything but hard times.
Come in, sheets are clean,

15   fall down on me for one more year
and we can blast another hole in ourselves without a sound.

Since poems' titles are chosen very carefully, we can begin to understand this poem by noticing, in the title, that it is about an anniversary. We may have in our minds certain associations with anniversaries, and we can determine whether those in this poem are similar to our own. The first idea of the poem, written in sentence form, is "You raise the ax, the block of wood screams in half, while I lift the sack of flour and carry it into the house." The speaker is describing two actions: the partner's and the speaker's. If you were to write this in your own words, you might say, "The partner is chopping wood and the speaker is carrying flour into the house." This reduces the first idea of the poem to its most basic form, but it opens a door to understanding what is going on: two people are working at providing heat and food for their existence.

The next idea seems fairly straightforward as well, but perhaps it raises some questions. You might write, "The speaker is not afraid of the ax blade." You might also ask, "Why isn't the speaker afraid of something that could hurt him or her?" "Has the partner actually pointed the blade at the speaker's head, or is the speaker seeing the partner's swinging of the ax as a potentially violent act? Has there been violence between the two before?"

In the third idea, we are introduced to a child—presumably the couple's son. You might write, "If the speaker were dead, the partner could hunt with the son." You might ask, "Why can't the partner hunt with the son while the speaker is alive? Is there a rivalry between the son and the speaker for the partner's attention? Does kissing (and sex) help keep the two adults together?"

It is the questions inspired by the paraphrasing, rather than the rewritten lines themselves, that really help us make progress with this poem. We connect with the ideas in the poem by asking, "Why?" "What if?" etc. If we were to continue in this way to the end of the poem, we would have a series of questions developed from our increasing under-standing as we made more and more connections. If we then went back to the poem and looked at the actual words used to express its ideas, we might find some answers to our questions and make even more progress in understanding the poem's meaning.

By communicating with a poem on our own terms, we are able to make some sense of it and ultimately to appreciate the detail included in it by the poet. By making connections with and within the poem, we can begin to make its meaning come alive.

## YOUR TURN

Rewrite the ideas in Ai's poem (or another one) and communicate with them. Try to produce a list of questions, find as many answers as you can by making connections, and then compare your results with someone else's viewpoint.

# DOOR #4
## WHAT MAKES THIS POEM WORK?

# Organization of Ideas

## YOUR PERCEPTION

Have you ever tried to convince your parents that you need something (or your kids that they don't)? How do you plan your argument? In which order do you present the points—strongest first or strongest last? Are you usually successful?

## THE CONCEPT

Poets too try to present their ideas in a progression that will be successful. It is no accident that their points are made in a particular order: they too can place a central idea at the beginning or the end of a poem and strategically include details that will support it. Poets try to lead their readers through their impressions of the world by communicating clearly, and they understand that, as with all genres of writing, the structure of their ideas will affect their readers' comprehension.

In the following poem, Countee Cullen's central idea is that the experience of one isolated moment, or one word, can make a stronger impression on memory than months of experience of a particular person or place. He begins the poem with the child speaker's pleasant description of visiting a city and meeting a boy his or her own age. Contrasting with this rather ordinary scene is the immediately following offensive word and its effect on the speaker. Had Cullen reversed the order of these ideas, the shock created by the contrast, and therefore the success of the poem, would have been lessened.

# Incident

*For Eric Walrond*

Once riding in old Baltimore,
    Heart-filled, head-filled with glee,
I saw a Baltimorean
    Keep looking straight at me.

5    Now I was eight and very small,
    And he was no whit bigger,
And so I smiled, but he poked out
    His tongue, and called me, "Nigger."

I saw the whole of Baltimore
10    From May until December;
Of all the things that happened there
    That's all that I remember.

by Countee Cullen

# THE PORTRAIT

by Stanley Kunitz

My mother never forgave my father

for killing himself,

especially at such an awkward time

and in a public park,

that spring                                                    5

when I was waiting to be born.

She locked his name

in her deepest cabinet

and would not let him out,

though I could hear him thumping.                              10

When I came down from the attic

with the pastel portrait in my hand

of a long-lipped stranger

with a brave moustache

and deep brown level eyes,                                     15

she ripped it into shreds

without a single word

and slapped me hard.

In my sixty-fourth year

I can feel my cheek                                            20

still burning.

In this poem, Stanley Kunitz comes to a conclusion similar to Cullen's in the previous poem—about the strong impact of a particular, isolated event on memory—but this time, it is not the central theme of the poem. The speaker's memory of being slapped by his or her mother is only one of a number of details included to help explain the mother's response to her husband's suicide. Here, the central theme seems to be the lasting effect that a dead, as well as a living, parent's actions can have on a child. If Kunitz had stated this theme explicitly rather than showing it with imagery throughout the poem, the message would have been weakened. Instead, he immediately catches our attention with the image of the father's suicide and the mother's response. Having this background information, we then read more about the mother's attempt to forget about the father and her angry reaction when the child finds his portrait. If any of these details had not been included, or had been presented in a different sequence, their impact would have been lost.

## YOUR TURN

Using the keys presented so far in this text, read the following poem and identify its ideas (be sure to substitute "you" for "thee" and "thou" and "your" for "thy," at least the first time through!). Try to identify the central (most important) theme and think about how the details in the poem support it. If Donne had expressed the ideas in a different order, would the poem have been as effective?

# DEATH BE NOT PROUD

### by John Donne

Death, be not proud, though some have callèd thee

Mighty and dreadful, for thou art not so;

For those whom thou think'st thou dost overthrow

Die not, poor Death, nor yet canst thou kill me.

5      From rest and sleep, which but thy pictures be,

Much pleasure; then from thee much more must flow,

And soonest our best men with thee do go,

Rest of their bones, and soul's delivery.

Thou art slave to Fate, Chance, kings, and desperate men,

10      And dost with Poison, War, and Sickness dwell,

And poppy or charms can make us sleep as well

And better than thy stroke; why swell'st thou then?

One short sleep past, we wake eternally,

And death shall be no more; Death, thou shalt die.

# Rhyme and Rhythm

## YOUR PERCEPTION

Can you still remember any of the rhymes you learned as a child? Was there one for skipping rope or playing another game? Have you ever thought about why humans respond strongly to rhythm and rhyme?

## THE CONCEPT

Some say that the natural processes of our bodies provide personal rhythms for each of us and make us attuned to other patterns of beat and sound around us. When we respond to the beat of a poem, for instance, they say it is because we are recognizing a natural pattern that occurs elsewhere in the earth as well as in our personal rhythms. Whatever the reason, humans do seem to notice and respond to rhythm and rhyme in many forms, including poetry. Often, the study of poetry begins with analysis of its structure and technique, and this involves learning about rhyme schemes and metric patterns. This text has instead focused so far on the words and ideas in poetry, but it wouldn't be complete without at least a mention of some of the devices (techniques) poets use when they write poems that follow formal conventions. The use of rhythm and rhyme, for example, supports a poem's ideas and represents another option open to poets when they choose ways to express their observations.

# One Perfect Rose

by Dorothy Parker

A single flow'r he sent me, since we met.
    All tenderly his messenger he chose;
Deep-hearted, pure, with scented dew still wet –
    One perfect rose.

5        I knew the language of the floweret;
    "My fragile leaves," it said, "his heart enclose."
Love long has taken for his amulet
    One perfect rose.

Why is it no one ever sent me yet
10      One perfect limousine, do you suppose?
Ah no, it's always just my luck to get
    One perfect rose.

Dorothy Parker uses a formal pattern of both rhyme and rhythm in this poem. In each group of four lines, the first and third lines rhyme, as do the second and fourth. Most of the lines follow the rhythmic pattern called iambic pentameter (five "da-**dahs**" per line, or five pairs of syllables with the second one accented). The use of these patterns makes the poem sound traditional and formal, yet this formal structure can also be seen as part of the poem's humour. When the speaker suggests that she would like the traditional flower to be replaced with a modern limousine, she could be suggesting that the formal, flowery language of traditional poetry should be replaced as well.

# If This Be Love

## by Henry Constable

To live in hell, and heaven to behold;

To welcome life, and die a living death;

To sweat with heat, and yet be freezing cold;

To grasp at stars, and lie the earth beneath;

To tread a maze that never shall have end;                    5

To burn in sighs, and starve in daily tears;

To climb a hill, and never to descend;

Giants to kill, and quake at childish fears;

To pine for food, and watch the Hesperian tree;

To thirst for drink, and nectar still to draw;               10

To live accurst, whom men hold blest to be;

And weep those wrongs which never creature saw;

If this be love, if love in these be founded

My heart is love, for these in it are grounded.

Henry Constable uses a traditional sonnet format in this poem: if you divide the first twelve lines into groups of four, the first and third lines rhyme, as do the second and fourth lines. The last two rhyming lines stand on their own. In the poem, Constable provides a definition of love by listing many contradictions. Each of these begins with the word "To," and each also has a similar rhythm (iambic pentameter again). The similar rhythmic and rhyming structure of the contradictions gives consistency to the poem's ideas and helps us, as readers, to follow the list. When we reach the last two lines, and Constable gives us the "punch line," or the central idea of the poem, we are expecting it and need it to put the composite definition of love, with all its contradictions, into context. Constable's choice of structure and rhyme scheme thus supports the ideas he expresses in his poem.

## YOUR TURN

Identify the rhythm and rhyme patterns in two poems. Even if you don't know the formal names for the patterns, explain how they work (i.e., which lines rhyme with each other, and how many syllables and accents are in each line). Then make some connections between the patterns and the ideas expressed in the poem: how do the rhythm and rhyme support the poem's central ideas?

# Word Choice and Sound

## YOUR PERCEPTION

If you didn't know what the word "squish" meant, what would you guess? How about the word "patter"? If "hirp" was a word, what meaning would you give it?

## THE CONCEPT

We have talked about listening to rhyme and rhythm in groups of words, but individual words can contribute to the way a poem sounds as well. Some words in English make sounds similar to their meanings. "Squish," for instance, sounds like something having the liquid pushed out of it. Poets' use of words that make sounds themselves is called "onomatopoeia." Because words can be chosen for their sounds as well as their meanings in poetry, it is important to recognize techniques such as onomatopoeia. The sense of sound, from many sources in a poem, can contribute significantly to its meaning.

In the following short poem about the ocean in winter, John Updike uses several words that create ocean sounds. "Scud-thumper," "shrub-ruster," and "sky-mocker" are all pairs of words in which the first word begins with "s" and the second, with another consonant. While each word pair means something, reminding us of an effect the ocean can have, each pair also contributes to the sounds that push and spread (like ocean waves) in the poem. Updike uses his words in two ways: to provide a visual image of the ocean and to encourage us to use our imaginations to hear its sound.

# Winter Ocean

by John Updike

Many-maned scud-thumper, tub

of male whales, maker of worn wood, shrub-

ruster, sky-mocker, rave!

portly pusher of waves, wind-slave.

# Night Driving

**by Adam Sol**


No one selling cherries

         at roadside kiosks,

no whitetails chewing

         gravel, forelegs pointed

at the guardrail.                                   5

         Minivans kick up

what's left of the rain,

         passing. Yellow

divider uneven, slanted.

         Engine a conch shell.            10

We are headed north

         at a speed familiar to baseballs.

Trees hiss with crickets

         or wind, flash

brights at oncoming trucks                  15

         to warn them of speed traps. She sleeps

curled against the window,

         her prerogative

after our snarls and whispers.

         We lean left,                    20

I right us. She doesn't stir

         as we rush over a bridge,

the rumble of the road

         suddenly a Gregorian chant. If I turn

the wheel two inches, this                25

         argument will be over.

                             Two inches.

In this poem, Adam Sol gives us a driver's impressions after arguing with a woman in the car's passenger seat. The poet's word choice contributes to the sense of tension in the poem after the woman has fallen asleep with the argument still unsettled. Each image and idea is expressed in a fairly short, terse phrase: the minivans "kick up," trees "hiss," the couple has exchanged "snarls and whispers," the car "rushes" and the road "rumbles." All of these harsh sounds hint at the undercurrent between the couple: although the woman is sleeping, the argument continues. Sol uses sound to intensify his description of the tense atmosphere in the car, and by the end of the poem, we can sense the driver's frustration. It is also interesting to note the layout of the two halves of this poem: the alternating phrases on different lines suggest the sounds of an argument in which short bursts of speech enter the atmosphere but do not meet or interact in conversation. Sol's word choice thus encourages us to notice the sound, the meaning, and the visual structure of the words in this poem.

## YOUR TURN

Find a poem that uses specific words to contribute to its sound. Think about both the meaning and the sounds of the words and connect them to the central theme of the poem.

# Alliteration

## YOUR PERCEPTION

Have you ever tried to repeat a tongue-twister, a group of words that begins with the same sound? Here's a popular one (try reading it as quickly as you can): Peter Piper picked a peck of pickled peppers. If Peter Piper picked a peck of pickled peppers, where's the peck of pickled peppers Peter Piper picked?

## THE CONCEPT

Another way that poets can organize sound in their work is to use repetition. "Alliteration," a frequently used form of repetition, consists of repeating sounds at the beginnings of words, as in the line, "*Peter Piper picked a peck of pickled peppers*." Alliteration is often used to create momentum and emphasize the theme of a poem. Along with rhyme, rhythm, and specific word choice, alliteration gives a poet another tool with which to express ideas.

In the first lines of the following poem, F. R. Scott employs alliteration in his use of words beginning with "s" to describe the Laurentian Shield. This may seem strange since Scott is talking about rock, and the "s" sound often suggests softness, fluidity, and motion. He sees this land, however, as full of so much life that he personifies it (gives it human characteristics): it stares, endlessly repeats, and leans. Given this image of life within the rocky land and still lakes, Scott's repeated use of "s" words to describe them makes sense. By the end of the poem (second stanza above), Scott talks about the life that people will create on the Shield in the future (the poem was written in 1954). Here we can see that Scott's use of alliteration in the first stanza to suggest life within the land ultimately supports his theme of human life emerging from that land in the final stanza.

# *From* Laurentian Shield

### by F.R. Scott

Hidden in wonder and snow, or sudden with summer,
This land stares at the sun in a huge silence
Endlessly repeating something we cannot hear.
Inarticulate, arctic,
5   Not written on by history, empty as paper,
It leans away from the world with songs in its lakes
Older than love, and lost in the miles.
. . .

But a deeper note is sounding, heard in the mines,
The scattered camps and the mills, a language of life,
10   And what will be written in the full culture of occupation
Will come, presently, tomorrow,
From millions whose hands can turn this rock into children.

# Blackberry Eating

## by Galway Kinnell

I love to go out in late September

among the fat, overripe, icy, black blackberries

to eat blackberries for breakfast,

the stalks very prickly, a penalty

they earn for knowing the black art                                5

of blackberry-making; and as I stand among them

lifting the stalks to my mouth, the ripest berries

fall almost unbidden to my tongue,

as words sometimes do, certain peculiar words

like *strengths* or *squinched*,                                10

many-lettered, one-syllabled lumps,

which I squeeze, squinch open, and splurge well

in the silent, startled, icy, black language

of blackberry-eating in late September.

Here, Galway Kinnell compares eating blackberries to language, so we would expect him to play with specific words and their sounds in this poem. In the first six lines, he uses alliteration by repeating the "bl" sound five times. Making that sound requires us to move our mouths and tongues in ways that we might if we were eating, which is the action being described in the poem. The use of alliteration here thus helps us to connect more strongly with the ideas in the poem. Later in the poem, Kinnell uses a number of words beginning with "s" ("stand," "stalks," "sometimes," "strengths," squinched, etc.), giving us a sense of the sounds associated with eating berries. The use of repetition in this poem emphasizes important ideas and encourages us to read the poem more than once. What other connections can you make between the poet's use of alliteration and the poem's meaning?

## YOUR TURN

Find a poem that contains alliteration. Analyze its central theme and make connections between the theme and the poet's use of alliteration.

# Making Connections: Format and Sound

## YOUR PERCEPTION

Do you like to have someone read aloud to you? Do you like to read aloud? Have you ever tried reading either your own or someone else's writing aloud in order to help you focus on details?

## THE CONCEPT

Many people enjoy hearing the words of stories, familiar or new, brought to life by someone who reads with expression. Reading your own writing aloud can also be useful as a way to catch inconsistencies or errors. Reading others' writing aloud can help us to find meaning in the writing and help us to notice detail that we might miss by reading silently. We can certainly appreciate poetry when we read it silently, but because of its sound components, when it is read aloud, it seems to become more alive. Door #4 has talked about the organization of ideas, rhyme and rhythm, word choice and sound, and alliteration in poetry. Each of these aspects is much easier to identify in a poem that is heard as well as seen.

# Pity me not
### by Edna St. Vincent Millay

Pity me not because the light of day

At close of day no longer walks the sky;

Pity me not for beauties passed away

From field and thicket as the year goes by;

5  Pity me not the waning of the moon,

Nor that the ebbing tide goes out to sea,

Nor that a man's desire is hushed so soon,

And you no longer look with love on me.

This have I known always: Love is no more

10  Than the wide blossom which the wind assails,

Than the great tide that treads the shifting shore,

Strewing fresh wreckage gathered in the gales:

Pity me that the heart is slow to learn

What the swift mind beholds at every turn.

Try reading this poem aloud, observing the punctuation marks that indicate the organization of its ideas. Notice repetitions such as the word "pity," and identify the poem's central theme. Edna St. Vincent Millay suggests that her speaker should be pitied for only one thing: what is it?

Read the poem aloud again, and listen for rhyme and rhythmic patterns. Because this is a sonnet, we can identify three sets of four lines and then one pair of lines at the end, all with a consistent rhyme and rhythm. How do these elements contribute to the organization and meaning of the poem?

Are the descriptions in this poem particularly strong? Does any specific choice of words stand out? If so, how do these words support and emphasize the poem's theme? Finally, is there any alliteration in the poem? Can you identify its purpose?

Obviously, not every poet uses every technique we have discussed in every poem. Some poets seem to use many devices, while others seem to use none at all. Learning to read poetry actively includes learning to recognize and appreciate the technical decisions poets make.

# Richard Cory

by Edwin Arlington Robinson

Whenever Richard Cory went down town,
We people on the pavement looked at him:
He was a gentleman from sole to crown,
Clean favored, and imperially slim.

And he was always quietly arrayed,                    5
And he was always human when he talked;
But still he fluttered pulses when he said,
"Good-morning," and he glittered when he walked.

And he was rich – yes, richer than a king –
And admirably schooled in every grace:              10
In fine, we thought that he was everything
To make us wish that we were in his place.

So on we worked, and waited for the light,
And went without the meat, and cursed the bread;
And Richard Cory, one calm summer night,          15
Went home and put a bullet through his head.

What do you notice when you read this poem aloud? What stands out? Who are the "we" in the poem, and how does Edwin Arlington Robinson compare them to Richard Cory? What is the poem's theme?

How does the structure of the poem contribute to the contrast between the people in the town and Richard Cory? Which words emphasize this difference? Can you identify any other poetic devices?

Try reading the poem in various ways: quickly and slowly, loudly and quietly. Which variations bring the words to life? Which words need to be emphasized, and which phrases need to be kept together? Emphasizing details in your reading of a poem aloud can help the listeners, as well as you, to understand it more easily.

## YOUR TURN

Choose a poem to read aloud to your class. Prepare your reading by noticing the details of organization and sound that are in the poem, and include appropriate emphasis of these to make the poem come alive for your listeners. When you have finished your reading, you may want to hand out copies of the poem and ask the class to comment on what they did and didn't understand from your reading. Which details of a poem need to be both read and heard to be fully understood?

# DOOR #5

## TAKING IT WITH YOU: HOW DOES THIS POEM FIT INTO THE WORLD?

# Time and Place

## YOUR PERCEPTION

Have you ever wondered whether anything you study in your English course will relate to the rest of your life? Have you assumed that English teachers, and especially writers, live on their own little planet and don't talk to the rest of the world? Can poetry have any connection to reality?

## THE CONCEPT

Beyond its appeal and accessibility to individual readers, poetry plays a significant role in the reflection of history and culture. Because it is as firmly rooted in human experience as it is in imagination, poetry can speak as a record of history and act as a bridge among people. One of the elements that can help to achieve this communication is a poem's historical setting. A poet can be moved by an event in history and write her impressions of it, or she can describe what it is like to be in a particularly significant location. In order to understand a poem that is situated very specifically, we need to focus on the details of its setting.

The following excerpts from Galway Kinnell's poem give us a strong sense of the horror experienced by those who saw the twin towers collapse in New York City on September 11, 2001. Although it is difficult to find anyone who doesn't know smething about that infamous event, Kinnell's poem offers us a detailed view that few people experienced. By locating the action in specific parts of New York (lower Fifth Avenue, the Arch, Washington Square Park), and describing the day's events in such precise detail, Kinnell invites us into the setting and contributes to the cultural record of these significant moments in history.

# *From*
# When the
# Towers Fell

5 by Galway Kinnell

From our high window we saw the towers
with their bands and blocks of light
brighten against a fading sunset,
saw them at any hour glitter and live
as if the spirits inside them sat up all night
calculating profit and loss, saw them reach up
and steep their tops in the first yellow
of sunrise, grew so used to them
often we didn't see them, and now,

10 not seeing them, we see them.

…

The plane screamed low down lower Fifth Avenue,
lifted at the Arch, someone said, shaking the dog walkers
in Washington Square Park, drove for the north tower,
struck with a heavy thud, released a huge bright gush

15 of blackened fire, and vanished, leaving a hole
the size and shape a cartoon plane might make
if it had passed harmlessly through and were flying away now,
on the far side, back into the realm of the imaginary.

…

In our minds the glassy blocks

20 succumb over and over into themselves,
slam down floor by floor into themselves.

They blow up as if in reverse, explode
downward and outward, billowing
through the streets, engulfing the fleeing.

25 Each tower as it falls concentrates
into itself, as if transforming itself
infinitely slowly into a black hole

infinitesimally small: mass
without space, where each light,

30 each life, put out, lies down with us.

# FACING IT

by Yusef Komunyakaa

My black face fades,
hiding inside the black granite.
I said I wouldn't,
dammit: No tears.
I'm stone. I'm flesh.                                    5
My clouded reflection eyes me
like a bird of prey, the profile of night
slanted against morning. I turn
this way – the stone lets me go.
I turn that way – I'm inside                             10
the Vietnam Veterans Memorial
again, depending on the light
to make a difference.
I go down the 58,022 names,
half-expecting to find                                  15
my own in letters like smoke.
I touch the name Andrew Johnson;
I see the booby trap's white flash.
Names shimmer on a woman's blouse
but when she walks away                                 20
the names stay on the wall.
Brushstrokes flash, a red bird's wings
cutting across my stare.
The sky. A plane in the sky.
A white vet's image floats                              25
closer to me, then his pale eyes
look through mine. I'm a window.
He's lost his right arm
inside the stone. In the black mirror
a woman's trying to erase names:                        30
No, she's brushing a boy's hair.

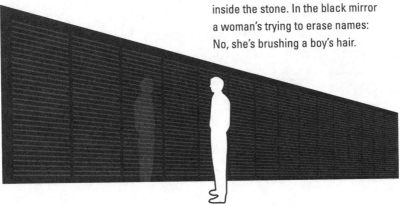

In this poem, Yusef Komunyakaa provides a veteran's impressions of his visit to the Vietnam Veterans Memorial in Washington, D.C. The poem explores light and ideas of reflection, and we can appreciate it on the level of that imagery. However, without understanding something about the Vietnam War and its place in North American history, and perhaps without seeing photos of the war memorial, we cannot fully appreciate the depth of this poem. What does the memorial look like? Why was it built? What was the Vietnam War all about? Finding answers to these questions and others can help us to place the poem within its historical context. Thus, expanding our sources of historical accounts to include authors' and poets' portrayals in literature can broaden our perspective and connect us more fully with the rest of the world and with its past.

## YOUR TURN

Research the factual details of either of the poems discussed, or find another poem that is strongly situated in time or place. Use all of the keys you have gained so far to unlock the poem's ideas, and then note how the details of its setting influence its overall effectiveness.

# Allusions

## YOUR PERCEPTION

You walk up to a table of friends, and they are talking about a movie they have all seen. If you have seen it as well, how quickly can you join the conversation? If you haven't seen the film, how much will you understand?

## THE CONCEPT

In addition to settings, poets can use allusions (references to actual events, people, places, works of art, etc.) to help express their ideas and put them into a context of shared experience. When a poet uses an allusion, he assumes that the reader knows about it and can appreciate its significance. If we skip over the details we're not familiar with in poetry—such as allusions—we may be left outside the meaning, unable to participate in the poem's connection to reality.

### The Three Emilys[1]
by Dorothy Livesay

These women crying in my head
Walk alone, uncomforted:
The Emilys, these three
Cry to be set free –
And others whom I will not name
Each different, each the same.

5

Yet they had liberty!
Their kingdom was the sky:
They batted clouds with easy hand,
10    Found a mountain for their stand;
From wandering lonely they could catch
The inner magic of a heath –
A lake their palette, any tree
Their brush could be.

15    And still they cry to me
As in reproach –
I, born to hear their inner storm
Of separate man in woman's form,
I yet possess another kingdom, barred
20    To them, these three, this Emily.²
I move as mother in a frame,
My arteries
Flow the immemorial way
Towards the child, the man;
25    And only for brief span
Am I an Emily on mountain snows
And one of these.

And so the whole that I possess
Is still much less –
30    They move triumphant through my head:
I am the one
Uncomforted.

1 A note identifying the three as Emily Brontë, Emily Dickinson, and Emily
Carr appeared with first publication of this poem in *The Canadian Forum*
(September 1953). Emily Brontë (1818–1848) was a British poet and author
of the novel *Wuthering Heights* (1848); Emily Dickinson (1830–1886) was an
American poet; Emily Carr (1871–1945) was a Canadian painter and author.

2 None of the three Emilys married or gave birth, whereas Livesay married
and raised two children.

In this poem, Dorothy Livesay's speaker compares herself to three
women named Emily. Fortunately, Livesay included a note with her poem
clarifying the identities of the three women she had in mind. Even if we
know the names of these famous people, however, but don't know anything about Emily Brontë, Emily Dickinson, or Emily Carr, the poem
won't make much sense. We need to have key information about the
three women's lives and their work in order to understand what they have
in common. With this information, we will be able to appreciate the contrast between them and the speaker. Without this understanding, we will
miss the central idea of the poem.

## Allegro

by Tomas Tranströmer
(Translated by Robert Bly)

After a black day, I play Haydn,
and feel a little warmth in my hands.

The keys are ready. Kind hammers fall.
The sound is spirited, green, and full of silence.

The sound says that freedom exists                    5
and someone pays no tax to Caesar.

I shove my hands in my haydnpockets
and act like a man who is calm about it all.

I raise my haydnflag. The signal is:
"We do not surrender. But want peace."                10

The music is a house of glass standing on a slope;
rocks are flying, rocks are rolling.

The rocks roll straight through the house
but every pane of glass is still whole.

The very first line of this poem presents the music of the composer Haydn as a comfort for the speaker after a bad day. Knowing what or who Haydn is will give us a key to the rest of the poem, where "haydnpockets," a "haydnflag," and several effects of playing Haydn are mentioned. Although the speaker refers to music in the sixth stanza (and therefore gives us a hint), we need to know what *kind* of music Haydn wrote, and an even more effective approach would be to listen to some of Haydn's music to get a sense of the power the speaker senses in it. Without this information, we won't be able to understand fully the poet's affinity for the music and therefore won't fully understand the poem itself. Other allusions are included as well: Who is Caesar, and what does he have to do with paying taxes? How are flags and signals related? Why does the poet compare music to a glass house unharmed by rolling rocks? Just a small amount of research will help us to understand the allusions and therefore read the poem from an informed perspective; we can then connect with it on a deeper level and begin to appreciate the poem's relevance to shared human experience.

## YOUR TURN

Research and explore the allusions in one of the two poems above or another of your choice. Think about why the poet may have chosen those particular allusions rather than others, and consider how their inclusion contributes to the central theme of the poem.

# What Does Poetry Have To Do with You?

## YOUR PERCEPTION

Have you ever felt really small? Do you ever look at the events going on around you and wonder how you can make any difference? Do you ever wonder about your purpose or the direction your life will take?

## THE CONCEPT

As we have seen throughout this text, poets write about topics that are significant to human experience. Just as we can learn about others in the world, we can also learn about ourselves as we read poetry. We have seen in Door #3 that identifying a poet's perspective on a particular topic can help us to understand the themes, or messages, of a poem. As we recognize those messages, we can allow them to influence us as we compare them with our own perspectives. Making a personal connection with poetry can therefore help us to discover more about our place in the world.

This poem can be read literally and can inspire an interesting discussion of travel and geography, but it also works on a figurative level, particularly because of the last two lines. If we look at the roads as options, and the choice of road as a decision we must make about a direction we will take in our lives, the poem can become relevant. We can relate it to a time in our own lives when we had to choose between two options: both options may have been attractive, but finally we were drawn to one rather than the other for a very personal reason. Perhaps now we can look at our lives in the present and see the results of walking down the road we chose rather than the road we didn't travel. Relating the poem to our own lives and comparing the details of the two possible options that Frost presents not only supports the poem's meaning; it also puts our own experience into a larger perspective.

# The Road Not Taken
## by Robert Frost

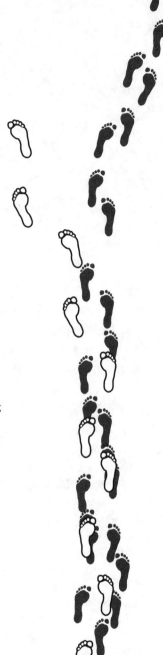

Two roads diverged in a yellow wood,
And sorry I could not travel both
And be one traveler, long I stood
And looked down one as far as I could
5    To where it bent in the undergrowth;

Then took the other, as just as fair,
And having perhaps the better claim,
Because it was grassy and wanted wear;
Though as for that the passing there
10   Had worn them really about the same,

And both that morning equally lay
In leaves no step had trodden black.
Oh, I kept the first for another day!
Yet knowing how way leads on to way,
15   I doubted if I should ever come back.

I shall be telling this with a sigh
Somewhere ages and ages hence;
Two roads diverged in a wood, and I –
I took the one less traveled by,
20   And that has made all the difference.

# THOSE WINTER SUNDAYS

Sundays too my father got up early
and put his clothes on in the blueblack cold,
then with cracked hands that ached
from labor in the weekday weather made
banked fires blaze. No one ever thanked him.    5

I'd wake and hear the cold splintering, breaking.
When the rooms were warm, he'd call,
and slowly I would rise and dress,
fearing the chronic angers of that house,

Speaking indifferently to him,    10
who had driven out the cold
and polished my good shoes as well.
What did I know, what did I know
of love's austere and lonely offices?

BY ROBERT HAYDEN

This poem talks about a relationship between a child and his or her father. As a child, the speaker viewed the father one way, but later on was able to appreciate some of his actions differently. If we think about members of our own family or others we are close to, there may be someone we view differently now than we did even five years ago. How has recognizing that difference affected the relationship? Hayden's poem, while it tells a very personal story, can help us to think about our own stories and perhaps even to re-evaluate the way that we see others' actions in our lives.

## YOUR TURN

Read through several poems until you find one that you can relate to personally. Identify a situation in the poem that is similar to a situation in your life. Compare the details of the situation in the poem to the details of your own situation. How are your experiences similar to the speaker's, and how are they different? Does the poem help you to see your own situation differently?

# Making Connections: Making Poetry Your Own

## YOUR PERCEPTION

Has your view of poetry changed at all since you started reading this book? Have you learned about any new ways to approach a poem? Do you see any purpose for poetry alongside the other genres of literature? Can you make poetry come alive for yourself and possibly even for others?

## THE CONCEPT

Poetry has been written by people of all cultures, genders, ages, and experiences for centuries. Our environments are rich with poetry: We see verses in greeting cards and in urban graffiti. We hear poetry in music and in the way our loved ones speak to us. We can encounter poetry of hate, violence, and horror. Poetry gives us an opportunity to focus on the details of living and to appreciate their significance. It uses words very carefully and emphasizes their power. Poetry is designed to say something to us, and if we're curious, we can follow its clues to understanding.

As we have seen, there are many doors we can open to find meaning and significance in a poem. The purpose of this text is to help students discover the doors and the keys that are most relevant to them and that lead them to a broader appreciation of literature. How can you put some of these ideas to work in your own reading?

The titles of Doors 2, 3, and 4 can act as key questions to ask when approaching a new poem:

1. What is this poem about?
2. What is this poem saying?
3. What makes this poem work?

Using these questions as a guide when you read poetry can help you to recall and use all the tools and skills you have developed. Even when you read a poem that seems difficult, if you are willing to work with it, you can find clues that will unlock its meaning.

# Mediocrity in Love

REJECTED

by Thomas Carew

Give me more love, or more disdain;
    The torrid or the frozen zone
Bring equal ease unto my pain,
    The temperate affords me none:
5  Either extreme, of love or hate,
Is sweeter than a calm estate.

Give me a storm: if it be love,
    Like Danæ in that golden shower,[1]
I swim in pleasure; if it prove
10    Disdain, that torrent will devour
My vulture hopes: and he's possessed
Of heaven, that's but from hell released.
    Then crown my joys, or cure my pain:
    Give me more love, or more disdain.

[1]Danæ, whom her father had imprisoned in a bronze house, gave birth to the hero Perseus after her union with Zeus, who appeared to her in a shower of gold.

1. What is this poem about?
   - Judging from the repeated words in the poem, what is the speaker talking about?
   - Is there any indication of whether the speaker is male or female? (For brevity in this discussion, the speaker will be referred to as "he.")
   - What is disdain? What are the meanings of "torrid," "temperate," and "estate"?
   - There are images of heat versus cold, and pleasant shower versus torrential storm. How are they expressed?
   - What are "vulture hopes"?
2. What is this poem saying?
   - Where do the ideas begin and end? What does each punctuation mark do?
   - The speaker seems to want some indication of emotion from an object of his affection. Why is disdain as acceptable to him as love? Why is he in pain?
   - How can someone be "possessed/ Of heaven that's but from hell released?" What is the meaning of the word "but" here?
   - What other insights can you gain by communicating with this poem?
3. What makes this poem work?
   - Find out more about the allusion to Danæ. What does it add to the poem?
   - Analyze the patterns of rhyme. Do they help to organize the poem's ideas?
   - Does reading the poem aloud bring out any relationships among words or ideas you hadn't noticed before?

Can you read this poem with more understanding now than you did the first time through? If so, you are using your knowledge and imagination to unlock meaning in poetry. This can be just the beginning of a lifetime of active reading. This text provides only a very basic approach to the appreciation of poetry, but now that you've taken some first steps, you can continue to unlock doors of further study.

## YOUR TURN

Choose a poem that is not easy to read. Challenge yourself to use the tools you have developed to read it actively and piece together its meaning and significance. Share your perceptions with someone else who has read the same poem, and be sure to acknowledge your progress and success!

# Glossary of Terms

**ALLITERATION** a form of repetition that uses repeating consonant sounds at the beginnings of words

**ALLUSION** a reference to an actual event, person, place, work of art, etc. which the poet expects the reader to recognize

**IAMBIC PENTAMETER** a rhythmic pattern that consists of five pairs of syllables in a line with the second syllable of each pair accented (i.e., five "da-**dah**s" per line)

**IMAGERY** specific words and phrases that create sensual impressions

**LINE BREAK** the end of a line (but not necessarily an idea) in a poem

**ONAMATOPOEIA** the use of words that make sounds that closely resemble the sounds the words represent (e.g., "squish" or "hiss")

**PERSONA/SPEAKER** a personality assumed by a poet to express a particular point of view

**PERSONIFICATION** the assigning of human characteristics to an inanimate object

**POETIC DEVICE** any technique used by a poet to express or emphasize an idea

**SETTING** a poem's location in time and space

**SONNET** a particular type of poem that has fourteen lines, usually written in iambic pentameter

**STANZA** a grouped set of lines in a poem or a song

**THEME** a significant message in a poem that expresses the poet's particular perspective on a topic

**TONE** the attitude toward a poem's topic suggested by a speaker's words

# Credits

# To Instructors

## RATIONALE

English teachers other than I may have noticed that glazed look in students' eyes when we mention the study of poetry. Often, the body language screams, "No! Run and hide!" I am not sure what some students think poetry *is*, but I am fairly certain about what they think poetry *is not*: interesting, relevant, worth studying, or accessible. Teachers of the reluctant need to meet students at the doors of poetry, usher them in, make them comfortable, and then ease into literary conversation and analysis. This guide for students begins on the doorstep of the study of poetry.

Even the least motivated and most inexperienced students can discover their own concrete means of enjoying and appreciating a poem. This brief guide invites students to begin their exploration by grounding it in their own knowledge. It provides simple, practical tools for understanding, rather than imposing the more overwhelming methods of attack and dissect. Once students accept the invitation to make poetry their own, they will become more ready and willing to learn the traditional vocabulary and methods necessary for vigorous close reading and analysis.

## CONTENT

This guide includes five short sections, or "doors," each centred around a question that will help students to focus on making connections with the subject matter and ideas within specific poems. In each section, keys to exploring the initial question are presented and demonstrated; students are then asked to apply these keys to poems of their own choice. The poems included in the text were chosen with accessibility, as well as diversity, in mind.

## APPLICATION

Students can use this text independently and then bring their explorations to class for discussion with their peers. Faculty can also present the material, demonstrate it in class, and then have students apply the concepts on their own as assignments. In whatever way this text is used, it is hoped that it will help students to enter the world of poetry on terms they can understand and appreciate.

## RESPONSE

This text was developed as part of my own teaching process. I would value feedback from those of you who use it in yours. I am particularly interested in student response to the content, including choice of poems and length and clarity of explanations. Please feel free to send responses to the address below so that we can continue the dialogue.

Cynthia Parr
University Partnership Centre
Georgian College
One Georgian Drive
Barrie, ON
L4M 3X9